Irish Paganism

An Introduction to Irish Folklore and Spiritual Practices

Table of Contents

Introduction

Pagans believe in the existence of numerous gods living in the world and the surrounding realms independently of humans. In other words, they don't live to fulfill the wishes of humans, create, punish, watch, evaluate, or even guide them. Like humans, these deities have plans and desires of their own, and why pagan religions view these deities as natural forces above humans but are not human-centric.

Upon reading this book, you'll learn everything about Irish Paganism. This book is an introductory guide to Irish folklore and spiritual practices to help you determine if this spiritual path is right for you. Whether you're thinking about adopting Irish pagan spiritual practices or merely looking to broaden your horizons and expand your scope of knowledge, this book is for you.

You will learn about the origins and history of Irish Paganism and how modern beliefs and practices differ from ancient ones. You will learn about the most prominent Irish magical creatures and their roles in lore and society. You will learn about the most distinct deities of the Irish pagan pantheon, gain insight into their traits and behaviors, and how they are worshipped today.

This book thoroughly explains the Irish pagan calendar, represented as the Celtic Tree Calendar and the Wheel of the Year. You'll learn why there are two calendars and discover the key festivals of the year. The following chapter offers a list of tools commonly used in Irish pagan magical practices and describes how they're used. This chapter guides you on how to incorporate magic into your spiritual practices as a beginner. Finally, you'll gain insight into Beltane rituals and come across step-by-step instructions on how to conduct several spells for a multitude of purposes ranging from love to healing.

Read on and delve into the intriguing and interesting world of Irish Paganism.

Chapter 1: Origins of Irish Paganism

Centuries before Christianity arrived in Europe, a group of people set foot in Ireland. They consisted of several tribes with their own culture, language, and religion. These people were the Celts. They weren't invaders but arrived in peace to mingle and co-exist with the people of Ireland. Religion was a big part of their lives. With the help of their priests, the Druids and the Celts spread their pagans' beliefs across the country. Although they didn't depend on the written word to record their history, much information in literary works gives us an idea of their ancient pagans' practices.

This chapter discusses the Celts and the Druids and their contribution to Irish Paganism.

The Celts

In 1200 BC, tribes emerged in Central Europe. The Greeks referred to them as Galatai or Keltoi, from where the name "Celts" was derived. The ancient Romans called them "Gallia," meaning "barbarians." However, this name didn't reflect who the Celts truly were and was an unfair representation of their culture and beliefs as they weren't, by any means, barbarians. The Greeks and Romans were at war for years with the Celts, so it made sense that they would have a biased opinion toward them and describe them as barbarians. In Greece, the Celts were known as savage fighters and heavy drinkers. While in Rome, there were always clashes between them and the Celts, and some violent acts by Celtic warriors resulted in cementing their unfortunate reputation. However, this can be regarded as a one-sided, and biased representation of the Celts exhibited during the war.

Although historians and ancient authors refer to them as the Celts, there is no mention of a word associated with them as a group in any literary work. They weren't given a name like the Vikings since each tribe already had its name and was ruled by a king.

Their societies consisted of the following:

- A group of intellectuals like the Druids, law experts, and poets.

- Brave warriors.

- High and low-ranking individuals who served each tribe.

These tribes were connected by their common culture, traditions, language, and religion. They left Central Europe, immigrating to other countries like France, Britain, Spain, and Ireland.

The Celts were powerful and hugely impacted many European countries, including Ireland. However, when the Roman Empire began expanding, the armies led by Julius Caesar invaded several Celtic regions resulting in the deaths of many Celts and the destruction of their culture. Great Britain stood tall against these invasions, making it a safe place for the Celts to call home. You can still find traces of their cultures in countries like Scotland and Ireland.

As a result of the Romans' failure to invade Great Britain, the Celts managed to settle there and spread and preserve their culture and religion. However, things changed with the arrival of Christianity. Many Druids were murdered, leaving Christianity as the main religion. However, the impact of the Celtic culture and religion in Ireland was so powerful it was impossible for Christianity to erase it from existence.

The Celts worshiped over 300 deities who were a big part of their religion and influenced their lives. They also believed that one's life didn't end by their death as their new journey began in the afterlife. Their belief in the afterlife was evident in their burial rituals. They buried all the dead person's essentials for traveling to the other side.

The Druids

The word "Druid" is derived from the Celtic word "Druwid," which translates to "strong seeing." This probably refers to the Druids' gift of prophecy. It might also be derived from the Irish Gaelic word "Doire," meaning "oak tree." The Celtic believed that the oak trees were sacred. They also considered them symbols of wisdom and knowledge, which perfectly describes what the Druids represented. The first records of the Druids were from 1 BC. However, it is believed that their cultural and religious influence in Ireland preceded these records.

The Druids were pagan priests among a group of intellectuals in the Celtic culture. Unfortunately, there isn't much that is known about them. However, interest and curiosity have always surrounded the Druids, which led people to heavily research their history while others merely speculated. Most information about the Druids came from the Romans, who interacted with them during the war.

Julius Caesar described the Druids as a group of individuals who were concerned with everything religious and sacred. He also stated that they had a keen interest in various subjects like education and astronomy. The Druids were very powerful and highly respected among the Celts. The ancient Romans, who feared the Druids' power could interfere with their control over Celtic communities, considered them a threat.

Looking at the history of the Druids, one can't help but admire them. They managed to establish strong and organized legal educational and legal systems. Even the Romans and the Greeks, who were some of the Druids' biggest enemies, couldn't help but record their veneration of them. They stated in multiple accounts that the Druids' scientific and mathematical knowledge was impressive. They regarded them as "noble savages" who were very educated, but their religious beliefs were primitive.

The Druids practiced their own pagan religion, referred to as "Druidism." It was a form of shamanic religion that focused on healing diseases and communicating with the spirits of the dead. As pagan priests, their role was no different from modern-day priests, which was helping people connect with their deities. However, some were also scientists, philosophers, judges, and teachers.

These pagan priests were held in very high regard among kings and the common people. Once they passed judgment, everyone had to obey. For instance, if someone broke the law, the Druids had the power to punish them by banishment. They could interfere during the war to prevent fighting and ensure peace. The Druids were treated differently from the common people as they were excluded from fighting in battles and paying taxes.

The Druids were ahead of their time as some of the first people in ancient history to practice gender equality. There was no difference between male and female Druids. Female Druids had the power to divorce their husbands, which was unheard of at the time. They worshiped gods and goddesses, and both were equally revered.

The Druids were divided into various sections, and the color of their robes defined their rank. The highest rank belonged to the eldest Druid, who wore a golden robe and was known for their wisdom and referred to as the "Arch-Druid." The lower-ranked druids were priests and wore white robes. The artistic Druids were mainly poets, and the new recruiters wore black and brown. They worshiped their deities in secluded and quiet temples. One of the most common worship places for the Druids was Stonehenge in Britain. Some historians argue whether the Druids built Stonehenge or not; some accounts state that they arrived in Britain after Stonehenge was built. However, Stonehenge is still a popular worshiping location among neo-Druids and pagan worshipers.

When Christianity found its way to Ireland, the Druids still found a way to co-exist with the new religion. Various Classic literary sources revealed that the Druids worked as magicians and healers after Christianity. It is safe to say that throughout history, the Druids have always managed to make a comeback, even in the modern age with the emergence of Modern Druidism. However, Druidry has never been as popular as it used to be during ancient Irish Paganism.

The Celts and Druids' Theology and Role in Irish Paganism

Paganism is a broad term that covers any belief outside Judaism, Christianity, and Islam. It revolves around worshipping more than one deity who usually looks more like a human than a divine being. Paganism focuses on revering nature, loving the earth, and uniting mankind under this love. Unlike the Abrahamic religions, the deities had human qualities and didn't exist only to guide and watch over humanity. In other words, they ruled the universe and all its creatures, but their existence didn't revolve around their creation. They had their own life, struggles, and stories that weren't associated with mankind.

The Celts were essentially pagans and, along with the Druids, brought their beliefs to Ireland, which still exist. They lived in Ireland for about 500 years before Christianity's arrival, which was enough time to cement their religious beliefs. Druidism was a polythetic religion, and the Celts spread the worship of their various gods and goddesses like Dagda, Brigid, Lugh, and the Morrigan across the country.

The Celts' Paganism brought a sense of unity to Irish culture. It was a diverse belief that didn't discriminate against the worship of any deities. The people could believe in as many gods as they wanted and would find total acceptance without judgment. It was a very welcoming religion that didn't set any rules, which was why many Irish people gravitated toward it. Seeing as the Druids highly revered nature, they influenced this belief in Irish Paganism. Druids hugely impacted Irish Paganism, and the religion is often referred to as Druidism.

The Celts and Druids were poets who considered nature sacred and believed in equality between men and women. All these ideologies were different from many other cultures at the time. They also believed that the divine is manifested in nature. The Druids didn't only see nature as the trees, sky, animals, and birds. It was something much more than that. Nature was everything in this world and the other world, meaning it also represented the realm of the spirits. The word "supernatural" didn't exist in Drudusim, as there was nothing above or beyond nature. The Druids brought this unique connection with nature to ancient Irish Paganism.

Many of the Druids' practices centered on deepening their connection with nature. They would spend time alone outdoors to feel one with the manifestation of the divine. To this day, the Irish and other pagans still highly revere nature and meditate to establish a connection with it.

It wasn't only nature that the Druids revered but also the spirits of their ancestors, whether they were dead family members or the ancestors that once shared their lands. Another belief the Druids brought to Irish Paganism was reincarnation - the idea that the soul's journey doesn't end with death but could be reborn in another human or other life form. Various cultures around the world believe in reincarnation and that a person's deeds determine what they will be reborn as.

The Celts introduced their own theologies and spiritual beliefs to Irish culture. Spreading these beliefs and preserving them was easy since

Ireland was out of the grasp of the Roman Empire.

No one can deny the impact the Celts and the Druids have on Irish Paganism, old and new. Thanks to the bravery of the Celtic warriors, they managed to immigrate to Ireland and protect it against the Roman invasion. They spread and preserved the religious beliefs that many people still follow today. They brought many theologies like revering nature, reincarnation, polytheism, and equality between genders. They introduced all these beliefs to a new culture that embraced and shaped it into what it is today.

Chapter 2: Paganism Then and Now

After the Celts brought their religious beliefs to Ireland, they changed the way the ancient Irish lived. Irish Paganism was more than just a religion; it was a way of life. They introduced the polytheism concept along with their various gods and goddesses. Polytheism significantly impacted the Irish people's cultures and traditions back then.

Since the Celts passed down everything about their lives orally, the surviving Irish mythology and folklore reflect how Irish pagans lived in Ireland. It is obvious that the Irish gods and goddesses were instrumental in their societies. For instance, if they failed to have a good harvest for one season, this could be devastating for the people of Ireland. For this reason, they had various festivals during certain times of the year to honor deities responsible for the harvest and seasons.

The Celts and the Irish pagans worked in trade, which was how both cultures intertwined with one another. The Celts didn't only introduce their religion to the Irish but also their language, weapons, and iron, which wasn't very common back then.

The most significant individuals in the Irish pagans' societies were the Druids and the warriors, with everyone else coming second. Many people were illiterate, which was pretty common in ancient societies. It was one of the reasons they passed down their legends and myths orally since most people couldn't read or write.

Seeing as the Irish pagans' highly revered nature, they didn't require temples to worship or communicate with their deities. Lakes, rivers, trees, and other natural sites were their places of worship. If they wanted something from their gods, they would sacrifice a valuable object as an offering by throwing it into the river.

Main Beliefs in Irish Paganism

Many beliefs shaped Irish Paganism, which was influenced by the Celtic culture.

Nature

Nature has been mentioned quite a few times due to its significance in Celtic and Irish Paganism. The Celts influenced the Irish pagans in how they honored nature. They were animists believing everything had a soul, like animals, trees, mountains, rivers, plants, etc. When humans deepen their connection with nature, they can bond with all its elements. Trees were considered the most sacred, which is why the ancient Irish pagans highly revered them.

Animals were also significant, as depicted in literature, religious beliefs, and art. The Irish pagans considered animals as messengers of the gods or messengers of their ancestors' spirits. Many ancient Irish legends featured animals as symbols of loyalty and bravery. Animals like boars were engraved on coins and helmets as they represented skill and bravery. Besides animals, water was also sacred, especially lakes; they believed the water from springs could provide healing.

The Irish pagans didn't believe the world revolved around mankind but that every creature was as significant. Therefore, they had to learn to co-exist together and live in harmony.

It's worth noting that the Irish pagans didn't worship nature; they only revered it.

Polytheism

Irish Paganism had various deities, and the people could worship as many gods as they wanted. No rules specified that you should worship certain gods together or prevent you from worshiping one deity if you worshiped another. Irish Paganism is a very flexible belief that lacks the rules imposed by other religious beliefs.

The Celts didn't base their deities on the ancient Roman or Greek religions. They had their own beliefs and gods, separate from other ancient cultures.

The Afterlife

They also believed in the afterlife, which is why they buried their dead with weapons and food, so they had everything for their new life. The "Otherworld" was seen as a place where the soul could continue its journey in a similar world, except there was no negativity, pain, or sadness. Death wasn't seen as a sad or terrifying event but as a continuation of life.

The Irish pagans believed the "Otherworld" was the eternal home of their ancestors' spirit and deities. In Celtic mythology, it was located either under the sea or under the earth. They referred to it by different names, like Mag Mell, Tir Naill, Tir Na Nog, and Tech Duinn. However, historians disagree here. Some believe that all these names refer to the ancient Irish "Otherworld," while others believe they are separate places.

The Irish pagans believed that the living could communicate or reach out to the spirits of the dead. For instance, they believed caves acted as gateways between the physical world and the other world, so they would leave food in caves for the dead to feed on.

Ancient Irish Paganism vs. Modern Paganism

After Christianity arrived in Ireland, Paganism slowly died out. However, it never ceased to exist. In the 1970s, Paganism in Ireland began gaining momentum again and was referred to as Neo-Paganism, Contemporary Paganism, and Modern Paganism. However, it didn't stop the modern Irish pagans from creating a sense of community similar to the ancients. For instance, a number of organizations are run by priests and priestesses to provide services to modern Irish pagans. Pagans in the US and Britain are bigger in number than in Ireland.

Neo-paganism was inspired by its ancient counterpart, borrowed from its practices relevant to the modern world, and forwent dated ones like animal sacrifice. They also believed that their deities lived in communities, the same as people lived in the physical world. Some Neo-pagans who didn't worship several deities believe there is only one god and one goddess. Both deities must be male and female, as modern Irish pagans are supporters of equality between genders.

Magic played a big role in modern and ancient Irish Paganism, and the Druids were known for practicing magic. Some people believe the ancient Druids practiced dark magic. Whether this is true or not, no one can really tell as we don't know much about them, and all the information is from the Romans and Greeks, who might have been slightly biased. However, modern Irish pagans follow an ethical code preventing them from using magic to cause harm. They use magic to heal, similar to the ancient Druids, who were considered healers. Their spells and rituals include chants and making magical objects.

Modern pagans, like their ancestors, highly revered nature and believed the divine exists in everything. For this reason, they treated the Earth with respect. Many neo-pagans and neo-druids are eco-friendly as they believe nature and the environment are sacred and should be protected. They connect with nature through various methods like meditation and prayer, similar to ancient pagans who also connected with nature through meditation and rituals. They shared other beliefs with the ancient pagans, like revering and connecting with the spirits of their ancestors, honor, responsibility, gender equality, magical practices, animism, worshipping Celtic deities, and celebrating the eight Celtic festivals.

While modern pagans and Druids try to practice an ancient religion in modern times, there can be a conflict between the old and the new. However, neo-pagans still remain loyal to their ancestors' beliefs; this was clear in the Neo-Druidry practice, which saw a revival in the late 20th century. Neo-Druids still follow in their ancestors' footsteps. For instance, many go to Stonehenge to worship their deities, like the ancient Druids.

Throughout history and until today, Paganism has always been a flexible religion. Modern and ancient Paganism doesn't include a book like a bible stipulates rules for its followers. Worshipers also believed that every person is responsible for their actions and beliefs; they don't blame fate or the gods for their circumstances.

There are eight festivals in the Celtic Wheel of the Year calendar that many neo-pagans still celebrate. They created their own "modern" calendar, quite similar to the Celtic calendar.

Modern Irish Paganism wouldn't have existed without ancient religions. They laid the foundations on which the modern pagans built their beliefs. However, like borrowing from any ancient culture, people often take what fits them in the modern world and leave behind what doesn't work today. Thanks to the religion's flexibility and the fact that it didn't have a book of rules like Christianity or Islam, it became easier for each person to customize their beliefs and practice Irish Paganism in their unique way.

Many ancient Irish pagans' beliefs are relevant to the modern age, like the equality of men and women. Neither the Romans nor the Greeks believed in gender equality and referred to the Celts as barbarians because they adopted this concept. Nowadays, feminism and women's right take center stage during any conversation, making ancient and modern Irish Paganism more relevant than ever. From day one, Irish Paganism has managed to create a community of acceptance that calls for gender equality and diversity, which are concepts many people have been seeking in the last century. This religion was indeed ahead of its time and featured many messages people might need now more than ever. For instance, connecting with nature and creating a sense of community are concepts many people need to adopt. We have been living behind our screens instead of connecting with one another and the world around us; it's no wonder this religion keeps reemerging, and people keep embracing it.

Chapter 3: Gods and Goddesses

The gods and goddesses of Celtic mythology were very influential and impacted every aspect of the Irish pagans' life. No one knows the exact number of Celtic deities, as much of this information was lost throughout history. However, it is believed there were over 300 gods and goddesses in Celtic mythology. This chapter covers some of the most significant deities in Irish Paganism and the most popular legends associated with them.

Dagda (The God of Life and Death)

The Meaning Behind the Name

This deity's name has different spellings: The Dagda, The Dagda Mór, The Daghda, The Dagdae, and The Daghdha. "Dagda" is Gaelic and was originally derived from the words "Dhagho-deiwos," which translates to "shining divinity." However, as the Celtic language evolved over time, the term changed to "Dago-deiwos," which Dagda was derived from. Dagda came to mean good, as in someone who has good skills.

Legend Associated with Dagda

Dagda, often referred to as the "good god," was one of the main deities in Celtic mythology. He was the chief god of the Tuatha dé Danann, a group of gods that ruled Ireland at one time.

When the Tuatha dé Danann were at war with the Fomorians, who were monstrous supernatural beings, Dagda tricked them into weakening their position. His wife Morrigan saw a prophecy that they would win the battle, but something terrible would happen. The Tuatha dé Danann indeed won the war, and Dagda, a strong and skilled warrior, fought bravely but was fatally wounded.

How Dagda Is Worshiped Today

Irish pagans worship Dagda by making offerings and throwing them in the fire. They also built altars in his honor, filled a cauldron with vegetables they grew, and placed it on the altar.

Symbols and Correspondences

- Life and death
- Magic
- Fertility
- Druidry
- Agriculture
- The seasons
- Skill
- Knowledge
- Wisdom
- A large cauldron

How to Connect with Dagda

Dagda was a generous and giving god, so the best way to connect with him was by making offerings. You can offer him Irish butter, milk, stew, pork, baked goods, and beer. Meditation is also an effective method to connect with him.

Signs Dagda Is Trying to Connect with You

Sometimes, the gods try to reach out to you for one reason or another. Maybe they want to provide guidance or warn you of danger. Watch out for these signs so you can answer the call.

- You will see him in a dream or a vision.
- You might see a cauldron in your dreams or in random places.

Festivals to Celebrate Dagda

Worshipers celebrate the Dagda on Samhain, which takes place on October 31st and November 1st.

Morrígan (The Triple Goddess of Battle and War)

The Meaning Behind the Name

The meaning behind the name "Morrígan" has confused scholars for so long since the first syllable, "Mor," has more than one interpretation. The first interpretation is Old Irish and means "phantom," while the second interpretation is Middle Irish and translates to "great." The rest of her name, "rígan," is translated to "queen." Therefore, Morrígan could mean the phantom queen or the great queen.

Legend Associated with Morrígan

The Tuatha dé Danann and the Fomorians faced each other in two battles. During one battle, Morrígan, with the help of her sisters Macha and Badb, used sorcery and made it rain fire on the enemy's head. She was one of the reasons the Tuatha dé Danann won the battle.

How Morrígan Is Worshiped Today

There isn't one way to worship the goddess of battle and war. You can worship her when you visit graveyards, practice shadow work, or during self-actualization.

Symbols and Correspondences

- Prophecy
- Shapeshifting
- Crow
- Wolf
- Raven
- Death

- Fate

- Fertility

- Destruction

How to Connect with Morrígan

An offering is the best way to connect with any deity. Meat is the best offering for this goddess, but you can give her anything you find appropriate. Certain rituals accompany making an offering to Morrígan. You must drink or eat a small part of it first; this shows the goddess that the offering is safe and isn't poisoned. Also, you should be in a quiet place with no distractions. While presenting your offering, ensure you say a prayer to the goddess. You can chant her name and its meaning (the great queen) a few times. Finish the process by showing gratitude to Morrígan.

Signs Morrígan Is Trying to Connect with You

It isn't always easy to determine whether a deity is calling on you. You might have to initiate contact to communicate with them and get an answer.

- Try divination, as it will show you if Morrígan is calling on you.

- If you feel that Morrígan is trying to connect with you, light a candle, pray to the spirits of your ancestors, ask them for guidance, make an offering, and pray to her. You will get your answer if she calls on you.

Festivals to Celebrate the Morrígan

Since Samhain is associated with death, it makes sense that it is a time to celebrate and honor the goddess of battle and war. According to Celtic mythology, a sexual union between Morrígan and her husband Dagda would guarantee abundance and a good harvest for the whole year.

Brigid (The Goddess of Fire and Poets)

The Meaning behind the Name

Brigid's Old Irish name was Brid, which has different spellings: Brigit, Bride, Brighid, and Brig. It is derived from the Celtic word "Briganti" and translates to "the high one." Scholars also believe the name could mean "to rise" and symbolize Brigid's association with fire and sunlight.

Legend Associated with Brigid

Brigid was the goddess who introduced sorrow to Ireland. During the battle between the Fomorians and the Tuatha Dé Danann, Brigid lost her father, the god Dagda, and her son

Ruadán. When Brigid arrived on the battlefield, she found her dead son. The goddess couldn't handle the pain of losing her father and son at the same time. She let out a high-pitch scream, which we now refer to as "keening." No one had ever wailed in Ireland or experienced grief before. For this reason, Irish women often "keen" or wail over their dead.

How Brigid Is Worshiped Today

Brigid's followers can honor her in group ceremonies. They pray for her during rituals when they welcome a new season. She is also the goddess many Irish pagans go to when they need guidance.

Symbols and Correspondences

- Fire
- Healing
- Water
- Motherhood
- Fertility
- Passion
- Serenity
- Poets
- Writers
- Sunlight

How to Connect with Brigid

Connect with Brigid by making offerings of bread, water, candles, coins, and blackberries. She will also appreciate the gifts you make for her. Creating a Brigid cross from rushes and hanging it over your windows and doors will reflect your loyalty to the goddess and protect you against negative energies.

Signs Brigid Is Trying to Connect with You

- Build an altar in her honor, pray, and make offerings to it every day.

- Light candles and wait for a sign in a dream or while meditating.

- Pray to her.

- You can make her an offering by writing her a poem or make her something with your hands.

Festivals to Celebrate Brigid

Brigid is celebrated at the Imbolc festival, which takes place on February 1st. During this day, people make offerings to honor the goddess and ask her for protection or healing.

Lugh (God of Justice)

The Meaning behind the Name

This deity's name is spelled Lugh and Lug. In ancient Ireland, Lugh was a very popular and common name. However, scholars can't agree on its meaning. Some scholars believe it is derived from the word "lewgh," which translates to "to bind by oath." Other scholars believe it could mean "light." Most scholars are more inclined toward the first interpretation because Lugh was associated with oaths.

Legend Associated with Lugh

Lugh was very smart and skilled and wanted to use his talents to join the Tuatha Dé Danann. When he reached the king's court, the guards told him he must provide a skill he could use to serve the king. Each skill he provided was already taken. Lugh, known for his sharp wit, asked the guard if they had someone who was the master of all skills. The guard said no and allowed Lugh entry as the master of all skills. Lugh proved himself to Nuada, the king of Tuatha Dé Danann, who trusted Lugh and believed he would make a great leader of his army.

How Lugh Is Worshiped Today

Lugh is worshiped by artists and musicians who are always looking for inspiration or creativity. Irish pagans honor this god by lighting bonfires, singing, and dancing.

Symbols and Correspondences

- Justice
- Oaths
- Nobility
- Rulers
- Trickery
- Thunderbolts
- Ravens
- Harps
- Crows
- Hounds
- Magic
- Spear

How to Connect with Lugh

You can connect with Lugh by saying a prayer you created. Offerings are also a great way to connect with Lugh. You can offer food like bread, milk, fruit, or butter.

Signs Lugh Is Trying to Connect with You

- You will see him or his symbols in your dreams.
- You could get a sign while meditating.
- You will have visions of him.

Festivals to Celebrate Lugh

Lughnasa is an Irish pagan festival that honors Lugh. Hence, the similarity in the names. This festival takes place on August 1st.

Cailleach (The Goddess of Winter)

The Meaning behind the Name

"Cailleach" is an Irish and Scottish word and translates to "old woman." "Caillech" is an Old Gaelic word, meaning "veiled one," from which the goddess name was derived. Throughout history, poets have called Cailleach by various other names like Burach, Biróg, Digdi, Buí, and Milucra. However, in literature, each of these names was a different individual, and each had its own story. For instance, Buí was Lugh's wife, while Biróg was another person who saved Lugh when he was a child. Scholars believe that Cailleach wasn't the name of a specific goddess but a term that referred to an old woman.

Legend Associated with Cailleach

One day, Cailleach, her husband, and her children needed shelter, so they sought the help of a group of people called the Glen Lyon. The people welcomed Cailleach and her family. During Cailleach's stay, the lands in the area were always fertile. When it was time for the goddess and her family to leave, Cailleach showed her gratitude to the people for letting her and her family stay by granting eternal fertility to their lands.

However, she had one small condition. The people must lay stones for her family between the Beltane and Samhain festivals.

How Cailleach Is Worshiped Today

Irish pagans worship Cailleach by praying to her or offering her food or whiskey.

Symbols and Correspondences

- Shapeshifting
- Hammer
- Thunder
- Storms
- Blue
- Snow

How to Connect with Cailleach

You can build an altar to honor the goddess and place any of her symbols on it. Make offerings and pray to her every day to establish a connection.

Signs Cailleach Is Trying to Connect with You

- You can see the goddess or her symbols in your dreams or visions while meditating.

- Call out to her if you sense she is trying to initiate contact and ask her to give you a sign.

Festivals to Celebrate Cailleach

There isn't a specific festival that honors Cailleach, but you can honor her at any time of the year.

Learning about the Irish pagan deities is an essential step you should embark upon before practicing the religion. Each of these deities has its legend that reflects who they were, which can help you understand them more humanely rather than seeing them as divine beings you can't relate to. They felt pain, fell in love, desired power, and experienced many more emotions. You can fear them like Morrigan, respect them like Dagda, or sympathize with them like Brigid. These deities are the reason Irish Paganism is still alive and strong. Even with the arrival of Christianity and its power over the world, people are still intrigued by these deities and try to connect with them.

Now that you are familiar with Irish gods and goddesses, you will discover their fascinating and magical creatures in the next chapter.

Chapter 4: Irish Magical Creatures

From leprechauns to enchanting mermaids, the lands of Ireland are home to numerous telltales and generational myths that gave rise to countless magical creatures. Magic and mysticism are intrinsic aspects of Irish customs and traditions. It was the people's way of making sense of the world, inexplicable occurrences, and the environment around them. This chapter explores the most popular mystical creatures in Irish Paganism. You will discover the story behind them, what they did, and what their appearances signified.

Abarta

Abarta is a mystical creature mentioned in The Pursuit of the Gilla Decair and his Horse. In this tale, Abarta wanted to be a part of the Fianna, hoping to dazzle Fionn mac Cumhaill. He approached the group of hunter-warriors and acted as a Gilla Decair, which translates to lazy maid or servant. The word lazy here doesn't apply to the servants but rather to the person they work for. To his disappointment, the Fianna were far from noble and chivalrous. They mocked whoever was not a member of the in-crowd.

Soon after, Abarta learned that his pay would be doubled if he owned a horse. The mystical figure summoned a huge, fierce horse for himself. It killed all the warriors' horses, which instigated rage, yet amazement, among them. Several esteemed members of the Fianna tried to ride Abarta's steed but failed miserably- Abarta was the only one who could control him.

Abcán

Abcán was either an ally or a member of the Tuatha Dé Dannan. This dwarf figure might have also been a deity. Abcán was thought to be the allotted harp player of the Tuatha Dé Dannan. He was an extremely gifted musician, and his music affected the behaviors and feelings of Cúchulainn. This dwarf poet could also transport people between the realms.

Abhartach

This mythological Irish ruler was a very cruel practitioner of dark magic. He was thought to murder and torture his victims for mere entertainment. Even though rivals killed him, he resurrected himself as a walking dead via his dark magic practices. He forced everyone under his power to make him a human sacrifice so that he could drink their blood. Even though he was constantly murdered, he never failed to come back to life until his subjects gave up.

Aibell

This ancient Irish goddess was considered the guardian of the fairies, the queen of the Banshees, and the protector of the Dalcassians. She played a mystical harp so beautifully that any mortal would die after hearing her music. She offered to play the harp for the Viking King Brian Ború at war. She warned him he'd die even though his army would win the battle.

Aos Sí

The Aos Sí are Irish fairy or elf-like beings. Some people believe they still live in their kingdoms beneath the lands of Ireland. According to other lores, these creatures live in mounds, hills, or entirely different realms. The Aos Sí are highly esteemed. They accept offerings as a token of respect.

Bánánach

The Bánánach were supernatural creatures who resembled screaming demons. They were attracted to warfare and haunted battlegrounds.

Banshee

A Banshee was a supernatural creature known as the "woman of the fairies" and foretold deaths by wailing or screaming during the night. Those who heard the screams of a Banshee expected one of their family members to die.

Bodach

A Bodach was considered a poor or elderly farmer who somewhat resembled the Banshees in function. People often took his appearance as an omen that something bad would happen. This mythological figure enjoyed playing tricks on everyone. However, he particularly loved annoying naughty children. He slickly slid into people's homes through tiny cracks to irritate them or keep them awake at night. Spreading salt around the home was believed to keep the Bodack out.

Cat Sìth

The Cat Sìth was a Celtic mystical fairy that took the shape of a black cat. It was larger than the average cat and had a white spot below its neck. It only walks on its hind legs when no humans are around. Many people suggest the Cat Sìth resembles Scottish wild or Kellas cats, who were dangerous but could've often been domesticated. According to mythology, this creature stole the souls of the dead who were not yet buried. It was believed that they lingered around funerals and burial sites.

Clurichaun

This creature is similar to a leprechaun. They are ill-behaved, passionate about shoe-making, and enjoy protecting treasures. Clurichauns and leprechauns like to plot pranks and sip on ale all the time, so people believed that Clurichauns settled in wine cellars and were short-tempered. While Clurichauns harm those who try to get rid of them (and their livestock), they are very loyal to families who treat them with respect.

Cù-Sìth

This hound-like creature was as large as a small bull and was thought to be the herald of death. The Cù-sìth was often depicted with either a white- or dark-green-colored coat. It was responsible for carrying a dead person's soul to the afterlife. If a person heard its howl, they had to seek safety before hearing the third howl, or they'd die.

Dobhar-Chú

This lake monster lived in Ireland and fed on meat. It looked like a giant otter and was hostile toward humans and other animals (particularly dogs). Dobhar-chú seldom attacked alone; they approached their victims in pairs or groups. If the first otter-like monster's attempt failed, the rest would intervene.

Dullahan

The Dullahan is a horseman without a head who rides a black horse. He is thought to be the personified form of the deity Crom Dubh. This creature meanders around towns, searching for victims to kill. His exasperating smile suggests that he finds joy in doing so. The Dullahan started journeying after sundown, which is why people drew their curtains shut. Those who looked at him lost their sight immediately.

Enbarr

This mystical being was depicted as a horse with a very flowy mane. This creature was linked to Manannán mac Lir, the deity of the sea. Enbarr floated gracefully over lands and seas and played a great role in Lugh's journey home.

Fairies

According to Irish lore, the fairies are among the first tribes to land in Ireland: the Tuatha Dé Dannan. Defeated in battle, this tribe had no option but to shrink so it could reside underground. The Tuatha Dé Dannan loved Ireland so much that they couldn't bear to live elsewhere. Many people still believe in the existence of fairies and blame them for inexplicable occurrences; this is why they wish to be undisturbed. However, they grant wishes to those who respect them.

Fear Gorta

We know very little about the Fear Gorta, as it is very mysterious. This mythological creature appears as a very skinny corpse with greenish, saggy skin. However, it attacks those who anger it and freely wanders the lands during times of drought. This mythological creature blessed those who offered it alms with prosperity and cursed those who didn't with poverty and hunger.

Fomorians

The Fomorians were supernatural beings who resided in the lands of Ireland. They were among the first races to invade the nation. They were portrayed as monster-like, ugly beings who came from the sea or emerged from beneath the ground. They had destructive abilities and were believed to take control over natural occurrences. Some people think the Fomorians are the embodiment of some natural forces.

Gancanagh

The Gancanagh is a very handsome male fay known for his hypnotic beauty, charm, and addictive touch. Even though he was rarely seen without a pipe in his mouth, he never lit it because he hated smoke. He was generally very flirtatious with all women but didn't touch anyone he wasn't attracted to. The problem with this magical being is he feared responsibility and commitment. He'd seduce women but was too afraid to start anything serious with them. Any more affection than he could handle would scare him away. He also got bored if he happened to be around one woman for too long.

Glaistig

This mythological creature took the form of a half-and-half figure. Her upper body appeared as a gorgeous woman, while her lower half was a goat. She was known as the Green Maiden because she wore a green dress covering her lower goat half. She had the power to appear beautiful or horrifying. Even though she was a rare sight, her screams were often heard.

Leanan Sídhe

This fairy belonged to the Aos Sí and was known as the fairy lover because she always searched for male mortal lovers. She was thought to possess extraordinary beauty and reside beside cemeteries because she typically targeted widowed men who visited their wives' graves. She usually offered to be the muse of many artists who often wound up dead from madness.

Leprechaun

Leprechauns are troublesome beings that like to spend their time in solitary. Their favorite pastime is shoe-making and executing devilish plots or pranks. While they may seem evil at first, these creatures can grant wishes to people.

Merrow

These mystical creatures are mermaids and mermen who need a magical cap to go back and forth between land and water. While mermaids were extremely stunning, to the point where sailors often found them irresistible, the mermen looked hideous, and no female Merrow accepted them as mates. Merrow men hunted the spirits of the sailors who drowned and kept them hostage beneath the waves because they were spiteful of their looks and how lonely they were. If a man were to fall in love with a Merrow woman, he'd have to take her magical cap to stop her from returning to the sea and persuade her to marry him. Otherwise, she'd sing an enchanting song that would forever capture the human's soul under the sea.

Oilliphéist

These creatures were serpent-like beasts who lived in the rivers and lakes. Many legends recount the stories of remarkable heroes who fought them. According to one myth, Saint Patrick planned to kill all the Oilliphéists he could find, so these creatures cut off the path of River Shannon. In another story, the creature killed Manannán mac Lir's granddaughter after she upset the Bradán Feasa, a very knowledgeable and wise salmon fish.

Púca

Púca could be translated into "goblin." This Irish mythological creature was a shapeshifter, meaning it resembled the appearance of anything it desired. However, a Púca most commonly appeared as an elderly man, rabbit, goblin, dog, goat, or horse. Even though these figures didn't necessarily take the forms of humans, they were perfectly capable of talking like we do. These creatures were greatly feared because they only came out at night when they would cause destruction. However, many people believe this was a mere stereotype as no one was ever harmed by a Púca.

Sluagh

The Sluagh are considered the most fearsome of all Irish creatures because they'll take the souls of anyone they encounter. Some people suggest the Sluagh particularly enjoyed killing people who found true love. These vile figures wandered around Ireland during Samhain, which is why people refused to light fires at some point in history. They thought it would attract the attention of the Sluagh.

Werewolves of Ossory

The legend of the Werewolves of Ossory most likely arose from the idea that ancient Irish warriors were thought to resemble wolves due to their wild haircuts and wolf skin garbs. By the 17th century, woodlands were still very abundant in Ireland, which meant that wolves weren't a rare sight. Many people killed them in return for sizeable bounties at the time.

One book called the Topographia Hibernica famously referenced the werewolves of Ossory. The book recounted the story of a priest who met a talking wolf in the woodlands on his journey from Ulster. Naturally, the priest was taken aback, but the wolf kept telling him not to be afraid. The wolf explained that he and his wife were under a 7-year-long curse that shapeshifted them into wolves. So, they had to let go of human life and assume the lives of wolves. If they manage to make it to the end of this duration, two other humans will take their place as wolves, and they could return to their old lives. The problem was that the werewolf's wife had fallen ill and needed the priest's help. The priest decided to give her the last rites. When the male wolf pulled her wolf skin away, he found an old woman underneath.

Irish folklore is rich in interesting mystical figures and enchanting telltales. This chapter explored the most prominent Irish magical creatures and the stories behind them. It offers plenty of insight into ancient Irish Paganism's customs, beliefs, traditions, and their way of life.

Chapter 5: Pagan Calendar and Festivals

The Gregorian calendar – the calendar used internationally in the modern day – is a relatively new invention. It was only introduced in 1582 as a replacement for the Julian calendar, introduced in 46 BC.

However, the Irish pagans used neither of these calendars when telling time. Instead, they use two different calendars – the Celtic Tree Calendar and the Wheel of the Year.

Celtic Tree Calendar

One way to think of the Celtic Tree Calendar is to think of it as a Celtic Zodiac. Like your Zodiac sign is based on your birth date and month, your Celtic Tree sign is based on where your birthday falls in the Celtic Tree Calendar.

This calendar is based on the moon and features 13 divisions or "months." Like the Zodiac, these months follow fixed dates rather than varying based on the waxing and waning moon. This method was chosen because there are a varying number of full moons in a year – some years have 12, and others have 13. If a calendar were based purely on the moon's cycles (lunar calendar), some years would have 12 months, while others would have 13. It would be difficult to relate that calendar to more popular calendars, like the Julian and Gregorian calendars.

It should be noted that, unlike the Gregorian calendar, the Celtic Tree Calendar does not start on the equivalent of January 1st. It starts on Christmas Eve.

Here is how the Celtic Tree Calendar is divided:

- **Birch:** December 24th - January 20th
- **Rowan:** Jan 21 - Feb 17
- **Ash:** February 18th - March 17th
- **Alder:** March 18th - April 14th
- **Willow:** April 15th - May 12th
- **Hawthorn:** May 13th - June 9th
- **Oak:** June 10th – July 7th
- **Holly:** July 8th – August 4th
- **Hazel:** Aug 5 – Sept 1
- **Vine:** Sep 2 – Sept 29
- **Ivy:** September 30th – October 27th
- **Reed:** October 28th – November 23rd
- **Elder:** November 24th – December 23rd

Each tree has magical properties believed to represent the people born in that period. Additionally, each "month" also has a corresponding Ogham letter, ruling planet and elements, and season.

There is some controversy over whether this calendar was followed by the ancient Celtic Pagans, as some scholars believe it is a modern invention. On the other hand, others believe the ancient Druids created it or pre-dated the ancient Celtic Pagans. Additionally, they believe it was the Druids who determined which tree would correspond with which division in the calendar and explained the magical properties of each tree chosen. Whatever the reality, it is a popular calendar among Celtic Pagans today.

The Wheel of the Year

The Wheel of the Year is a calendar based around the year's changing seasons. It represents how time was originally kept – through the seasons' movements rather than a system of days, weeks, and months.

This calendar is used in various pagan cultures, including Irish Paganism. According to Paganism's eight most important festivals, the calendar is divided into eight divisions. These festivals occur during the solstices, equinoxes, and midpoints between these days.

Using two calendars ensures that Irish Pagans can mark not only the most important days of the year (the festivals celebrated based on the Wheel of the Year) and have a coherent calendar that helps with telling time (the Celtic Tree Calendar).

The eight festivals celebrated by the Wheel of the Year are:

Samhain

Samhain is considered perhaps the most important festival of the Irish Pagan calendar. It is on October 31st (or, occasionally, November 1st) and celebrates the end of the season of light and the coming of the darkness of winter.

This festival essentially serves as a New Year's Day for pagans, as a celebration of the year's end and the start of the coming year. It is a way of giving thanks for the blessings you received the previous year, a day of reflection and memory of those lost in the same period and your ancestors.

It is the day the veil between the world of the living and the dead is at its thinnest. It allows communication between the living and the dead. For this reason, it is the most popular time of year to work magic involving communing with the dead, like holding a séance or performing divination magic.

Samhain was likely celebrated for centuries before the arrival of the Celts in Ireland. Some of the most important proof is the existence of the Mound of the Hostages, a passage tomb in County Meath built approximately 4500 years ago, far before the arrival of the Celts to Ireland. This tomb is aligned with the rising sun on Samhain, suggesting it played a key role in its celebrations.

Yule

Yule occurs on the Winter Solstice, the shortest day of the year, generally around December 21st in the Northern Hemisphere (the solstices and equinoxes are reversed according to hemisphere, so the Southern Hemisphere celebrates the Summer Solstice when the Northern Hemisphere celebrates the Winter Solstice).

Yule is the pagan midwinter festival and one of Paganism's most important festivals. In Irish and other Celtic traditions, one of the most popular ways to celebrate this festival was to decorate your home with evergreen trees. These trees represented the ability of life to survive the harsh winter, an appropriate symbol since Yule was also a celebration of the coming spring.

In Irish and Celtic Paganism, Yule celebrations celebrate the solar god's rebirth as the sun becomes brighter following the Winter Solstice.

One of the possible source words for the word "Yule" is "thoul," an ancient word for "wheel." The name "Yule" is a reminder of the changing seasons and a promise of the end of winter.

Imbolc

Imbolc is celebrated at the midpoint between the Winter Solstice and the Spring Equinox, generally on February 1st. It is a celebration of fertility, rebirth, purification, the promise of the future, and a reminder that winter will soon end, and spring is on the way.

The word "Imbolc" comes from a word meaning "in the belly" in Old Irish. It refers to pregnant ewes, promising a prosperous lambing season, and another reference to why this festival was marked as a celebration of fertility.

Imbolc was dedicated to the goddess Brigid, the Celtic goddess of healing, poetry, and (crucially) fertility. One way this festival is celebrated is by weaving dolls from stalks of corn, representing the goddess.

Ostara

The Spring Equinox is generally celebrated around March 21st. Ostara is a celebration of fertility, abundance, and the promise of Imbolc that is fulfilled by the dawning of spring.

As a celebration of fertility, this festival is linked with the rabbit, a well-known fertile animal. Other elements in Ostara celebrations include other baby animals, eggs, and flowers – all symbols of growth and fertility. Although Ostara is a relatively modern name for the festival, having been celebrated since the 8th century AD, it is likely linked to a much older spring festival whose name is forgotten.

Beltane

Also known as May Day, Beltane is held on May 1st and is traditionally celebrated as Ireland's first day of summer. The word "Beltane" means "bright fire," but the name of the festival could also be a reference to "Bel's Fire." Bel is a reference to Belenus, an ancient Celtic healing god to whom the festival was dedicated.

This festival was celebrated with fire (bonfires) and dancing (around the Maypole). It was and is a time of celebration and merriment among Irish Pagans.

Litha

Litha is celebrated on the Summer Solstice (the longest day of the year), generally around June 19th to June 23rd. It is known as Midsummer.

The festival represented a turning point in the year, as the days became shorter, and fall and winter would soon arrive. In some Celtic and

Irish Pagan traditions, it was a celebration of the day the Oak King handed his crown to his brother, the Holly King (the Oak King would retake his crown at Yule).

This festival was celebrated with feasting and bonfires. It was a reminder that while fall and winter were on their way, summer was still in full bloom and should be celebrated. It was a reminder that while the days grew shorter, it was only temporary, and spring and summer would return as the Wheel of the Year turned.

Lughnasadh

Known as Lammas, Lughnasadh celebrates the beginning of the fall harvest season. It is celebrated at the midpoint between the Summer Solstice and the Autumn Equinox, generally around the first day of August.

This festival was dedicated to the god Lugh (from where it gets its name), one of the most important Celtic gods, the god of justice and nobility, and the ruler of the Tuatha dé Danann.

The festival is celebrated with games and competitions such as horse racing, foot races, and fencing. These games brought the community together while honoring Tailtiu, Lugh's foster mother, who died of exhaustion after preparing the land for plowing.

Mabon

Celebrated on the Autumn Equinox (around September 20th to 24th), Mabon is essentially a version of Thanksgiving. It was a celebration of the second harvest and a way to honor the changing seasons.

It was a time to give thanks for the bounties a person was blessed with during the year. Also, a time to share the blessings with the less fortunate. Although the name "Mabon" is relatively modern, there's some indication that the festival – or one resembling it – has been celebrated for thousands of years.

The festival is associated with a range of harvest deities, who travel to the underworld in autumn, only to be reborn and return in spring. In the Celtic and Irish traditions, this deity was the fertility god Cernunnos.

Chapter 6: Magickal Tools

Magic in Paganism is closely tied to traditional Pagan beliefs, including folk and Celtic practices. While there is little concrete evidence of Pagan magic before the Middle Ages, there is plenty of lore affirming that even the ancient Celts have different magical tools incorporated into their practices. These were passed down to generations through oral traditions and evolved over time. In modern times, some practitioners still rely on ancient traditions, like following nature's cycle, performing major spells and rituals at each turning point, or enlisting nature's power for healing and divination guidance. Other contemporary Pagan witches use tools that became popular only after the 20th century.

This chapter teaches which magical tools to use in Irish Paganism and how. Animals and crystals are crucial in Pagan magic, so the chapter discusses these more in-depth. You'll also be introduced to the basics of Pagan magic practices, including setting up an altar.

The Magical Tools of Irish Paganism

The choice of tools depends on your preferences. However, here are some tools you can use in Irish Pagan magical practices.

Altar

Altars can be used for different purposes. For example, seasonal altars are set only to honor a specific season of nature and its associated spirits. Permanent altars are for everyday practices. Depending on their purpose, these can also be set up in several ways. Pagans mostly use crystals, herbs, and other tools for healing. To honor a deity or ask for their assistance, you need their symbol and plenty of offerings.

Staffs and Wands

These tools are typically used to channel magical energy to empower one's work or ward off malicious intentions. It typically happens before the work begins, so the practitioner can focus on the task ahead and successfully complete their work.

Candles

Apart from depicting the elements of fire, candles have several roles in Pagan magic practices. For example, their color represents your intention, or the flames can be used for cleansing other tools. Candles are often anointed with herbs, further enhancing their magical power.

Herbs

Besides anointments, herbs are essential for cleansing and providing healing energy. For purification purposes, dried herbs are burned, and their smoke is used to ward off negative influences. For healing, dried and fresh herbs can be made into solstices, tinctures, and other folk medicines and given to the injured or ill person. Small packets of dried herbs can also be used as protective charms.

Cauldron

Ancient Pagans magic practitioners associated the cauldron with Cerridwen, the deity known for its prophetic powers. Nowadays, cauldrons can have a similar purpose. However, they can also be used for offerings. Some use simple metal bowls to represent the cauldron.

Divination Tools

The Irish Pagan often employ simple divination tools, including fresh produce and other food items. Ogham staves were used, particularly in ancient times. Nowadays, some practitioners use pendulums and Tarot cards. Ogham staves are sticks inscribed with the letters of the Ogham alphabet and cast freely onto a flat surface. Pendulums are simple tools typically used to answer "Yes" or "No" questions when the practitioners sign them using their energy. Tarot cards can reveal much more about the future. They can be pulled one by one or laid out in a spread that requires a preset number of cards.

Pentacle

A pentacle is a mental or wooden (most often) object engraved with a magical symbol. Most Pagan magic practitioners use pentacles with a pentagram - the ultimate Pagan symbol of protection. It can help enrich your practice, provide a focal point when channeling your intention, and shield against negative energy.

How Animals and Crystals Are Used in Pagan Magic

Animals have always had enormous significance in Pagan practices for several reasons. In ancient times, they were part of the sacrifices, offerings, and rituals held for meaningful occasions, whether celebration, gratitude or assistance. Another way to incorporate animals into Pagan magic practices is through their spiritual significance. Animal spirits, spiritual guides in animal form, animal totems, and animal families are common in Pagan magical work. The souls of animals are often called on for guidance, divination, or other purposes. Whether this is the spirit of a pet you've recently lost, an animal you keep seeing in your dreams, or one that's been guarding you against the spiritual world since you were a child, they can be a great aid during your magical work and life.

Due to their unique magical correspondences, crystals are often incorporated into Pagan magic practices. They can be used for:

- **Protection:** You can store them on your altar and channel your intention to ward off negative energy while casting a spell, performing a ritual, or other magical practices. You can also use crystals as shields when casting a circle.

- **Empowerment**: By carefully selecting which crystal to use for each spell, ritual, chant, and talisman, you can enrich your practice and ensure success. You can also charge the crystal with additional power through elements of nature, the moon, or ask your guides to empower you through the crystals.

- **Divination**: By harnessing the power of crystals, you can sharpen your intuition and gain the ability to decipher divinatory messages. Meditate with crystal as you prepare divinatory work.

- **Healing**: Most crystals have a specific healing power to heal yourself or others. When incorporated into a spell or ritual or as a talisman, they can effectively heal the mind, body, and soul.

- **Attraction**: Crystals can help attract luck, new opportunities, love, and financial prospects. This purpose also works with charms, spells, and rituals devised to attract whatever you desire.

How to Practice Pagan Magic

There are many ways to practice Pagan magic. While Irish Pagan customs often call for traditional techniques, the approach to magical practices is highly personal. The tools and how you use them will always depend on your needs, preferences, and desires. Whether you prefer to work with spirits, deities, and other beings or opt for relying only on nature's power and yours, it is up to you. You can decide whether you wish to practice alone or in a group. The latter is great for sharing experiences and advice regarding magic or life as a witch. However, many find it spiritually gratifying and enlightening to achieve magical goals as a solitary practitioner.

Celebrating Nature, the Deities, and the Spirits

Many Irish Pagan magic practitioners hold rituals and celebrations to honor an important event in nature or a deity. Sometimes the two are tied together because the most influential deities of the Celtic pantheon are considered responsible for natural phenomena. The events are marked on a Pagan calendar called the "Witches Wheel of the Year." The largest events on this calendar are the solstices and the equinoxes. With the two solstices, you can honor the beginning of the winter or summer and the deities associated with them. With the equinoxes, pagans venerate the beginning and end of the harvest season (spring and autumn). Between equinoxes and solstices, there are periods when the divider between the worlds becomes thinner, which many pagan witches use for spiritual communication. Along with the major events, you can also choose to celebrate minor events, like the moon's phases. At any event, you can cast spells, perform rituals, or make charms that correspond with the occasion and your intention.

Setting Up an Altar

As a beginner, one of the best ways to commence your Pagan magic journey is by setting up an altar. While it isn't required to have one, novices and experienced practitioners find it helpful to have a sacred space. You can use it to channel your energy, focus your intention, and empower your work.

Set up an altar in an area where you won't be distracted during your work. It's ideal to have your altar face east, but if you don't have much space or if this direction doesn't work for you, face it in any direction. Use any flat surface, including tabletops, old chests, and nightstands - you will cover it with cloth anyway. If possible, only keep items on your altar (including the lower levels if yours have one) that correspond with your current intention.

When you've selected the space and the materials, you must cleanse them from negative energy. Smudging and cleansing rituals work best for this purpose. You can recite a quick prayer or invite a deity or spiritual guide to your altar. Once you've done this, start placing the magical tools on the altar.

Essential items you'll need to place on your altar include:

- A representation of a deity or spiritual guide: You can only do one or both, depending on who you are working with.

- Candles: These represent your intention, the elements, etc.

- Crystals: For the intention, empowerment, and more.

- Offering dishes: For seasonal and intentional offerings.

- Other bowls and dishes for herbs: Can also be used for other small tools.

- Symbols of season or precise intention: Used for specific goals and seasonal celebrations.

- Other items: decorations or personal possessions (yours, the spiritual guides, or something that reminds you of your intention).

Chapter 7: Simple Pagan Spells and Rituals

One occasion Pagan witches celebrate by carrying out rituals and enacting different spells is Beltane. Held on May 1st (in the Northern Hemisphere) or November 1st (in the Southern Hemisphere), Beltane is a sabbat marking the beginning of nature's new fertile period. As the seasons turn from spring to summer, the lands become green, and the soils get ready to start nourishing the new crops.

Beltane celebrations traditionally start the night before the actual holiday. However, many practitioners prepare their homes, altars, and themselves by preparing for the sabbat many days ahead. They celebrate Beltane through a broad range of customs. Most revolve around fertility - at this time, one can ask for fertility in all aspects of life. Others include asking for advice from deities, ancestors, and other spiritual guides - as the time is perfect for spiritual communication. Beltane celebrations can be held in groups or as solitary practitioners.

Here are some examples of rituals and ceremonies for celebrating Beltane:

- **Setting up an altar:** Decorating your altar with symbols of rebirth, fertility, and new life is a great way to honor this period. Candles are tools for symbolizing new life on an altar.

- **Reciting prayers:** Prayers of gratitude give thanks for the new opportunities and gifts you're about to receive. Prayers for fertility in different areas of life are also common. You can pray to the May Queen, the Horned God, or any guide you prefer.

- **Maypole dance:** After sunrise on Beltane day, young people dance around a pole decorated with ribbons. Each person has a ribbon in their hands, and as they move, they weave a pattern around the pole enveloping it in a sleeve. The ribbon symbolizes female energy, and the pole the male - their unity ensures fertility.

- **Sacred goddess ritual**: To celebrate the feminine aspect of nature, practitioners often hold rituals in the name of the Mother Goddess. In some traditions, one person dressed up as the goddess. While in others, the female ancestors are also remembered on this occasion.

- **Bonfire ritual:** This celebration takes place the night before Beltane when a group gathers around the bonfire to celebrate the May Queen and the Forest King. These two beings are represented by a young woman and a young man, who elaborately dance around the fire.

- **Planting seeds:** To celebrate the beginning of the new planting season, you can plant some seeds in your garden or a few pots if you don't have a garden. It's ideal for solitary practitioners.

Other Pagan Spells and Rituals

Apart from the Beltane celebration, Pagan witches can hold rituals and enact spells for many occasions and purposes. Here are some beginner-friendly spells and rituals you can try.

Healing Water Spell

Healing magic is part of many Pagan witches' repertoire, and with this simple spell, it can become yours, too. Besides the healing power of the herbs, this spell will help you gather additional energy - especially if enacted on sunny days.

Here is what you will need:

- Water
- Equal parts of rosemary, lavender, and violet
- Coffee filter
- A glass container

Instructions:

1. Boil the herbs in water over medium heat until the liquid is infused with their color and scent.

2. Drain the water into the container through the filter.

3. Put the container where it can bask in the sunlight and absorb its energy.

4. If the weather is inclement, put it in place you frequent. Each time you walk past it, take the container in your hands to infuse it with your powers.

5. Before sunset, take the jar to your altar, and recite the following:

   "By the herbs and by the power of the sun,

   health and I are now as one.

   I am now filled with strengthening energies.

Negative energies are now gone."

Use the water in your bathwater when you aren't feeling well.

72

A Spell to Attract Good Fortune

With this spell, you'll have positive energies to bring you luck, fortune, and prosperity in any area of life.

Here is what you will need:

- A candle
- A piece of string
- A small charm

Instructions:

1. Place everything on your altar and light the candle.

2. Tie the charm to the string and start swinging it above the candle flame while saying:

"As I pass this charm above the candle flame, may good luck and fortune come to me?

May I have wisdom, energy, wealth, and influence?

As this charm takes my power, it carries my wish to attract luck."

3. Repeat this three times, and wear the charm on your body or close to you to attract what you desire.

Ritual to Attract Love

To attract love, you can turn to Brigid, the goddess of healing and fertility. Needless to say, like any love spell, this one also only works if there is already a connection between two people. If there is, use the following ritual to invoke Brigid and ask her to forge a stronger bond between you and the person you love.

Here is what you will need:

- A red candle symbolizes love

- A representation of the goddess

- Matches

- A mason jar

- Paper and pen

Instructions:

1. Place the candle and the representation of the goddess in front of you on your altar.

2. Light the candle, and say:

"Beneath me, I feel the heartbeat of the stirring nature. May my life and spirit shine brightly as this flame does? With this flame, I call on you, Brigid. May you guide me on my quest to find the other part of my soul?"

3. Then, take a couple of minutes to focus on your intention. You can meditate, do deep breathing exercises, or any technique that helps you bring out your innermost intentions.

4. When you're ready, recite the following:

"Like Brigid, I shall be bold and attract the love I desire."

5. Once you have set your intention and said it out loud, write it down on paper. After, say this:

"May my heart be gentle. May my life enrich my lovers. May I love them fully and see what truly matters. May I live in harmony with them, as I do with nature."

6. Take the paper, hold it over the jar, and light it on fire.

7. Visualize your intention being sent to Brigid; she will help you make it into reality.

Rowan Protection Charm

A Rowan tree has powerful magic, and many of its parts are used for protection. You can wear the dried berries as beads on a necklace or create a charm or talisman. However, the most common way to use rowan for protection is to hang a few branches on your door around Beltane. It will protect you from evil spirits, fairies, and witches who want to harm you.

Here is what you will need:

- A few small rowan branches with berries

- A piece of string

Instructions:

1. Tie the string around one end of the branches. Make a loop when tying it off.

2. Hang the charm on your front door at least a day before Beltane night, so it has time to envelop your home with its protective magic.

Conclusion

As you have learned from this book, magic in Irish Paganism has a long-standing history. Irish Pagan practices were part of the ancient culture the Celtic tribes developed across Europe. One specific group of Celts, the Druids, made a particularly meaningful contribution to Irish Paganism. Despite being practiced in secrecy, several elements of Druidry can be found in traditional Pagan practices throughout history. Together with folk beliefs and ancient Celtic Theology, these elements have created a unique practice in Ireland.

The Christian Church banned pagan practices for several centuries, and much of the written evidence stems from Roman writers. While this made it harder for the belief system to survive, Irish Paganism (and magic) has seen its revival. Today, it has grown into a thriving community with practitioners from all over the globe. Contemporary practices incorporate elements from other religions while staying true to the ancient Celtic culture.

Ancient and modern practices rely on the reverence of the gods and goddesses of the Celtic pantheon, including Dagda, Morrigan, Aengus, Cerridwen, Brigid, Cailleach, and Lugh. Each deity has its magical correspondences, symbols, connection to nature, and the day of the Witches Wheel of the Year when they are celebrated.

Other practices of Irish Paganism include honoring the cycle of life, belief in the Otherworld and its inhabitants, journeying to and from the Otherworld, and divination. The Irish Pagan culture is rich in tales about magical creatures - some friendly, while others are feared. Some beings, like the fairies, are benevolent in nature but like to cause mischief, and if angered, they can turn against people.

The Irish Pagan calendar (represented by the Wheel of the Year and the Celtic Tree calendar) marks many festivals and sabbats, including Beltane, Samhain, Yule, Imbolc, Ostara, Litha, Lughnasad, and Mabon. These are celebrated with numerous rituals, spells, and large gatherings with feasts and offerings to the deities, ancestors, and other spirits.

Magical tools like crystals and animal spirits are often incorporated into these celebrations, accompanying the spells cast for protection, healing, love, fertility, attracting fortune, and more. These can be performed at an altar, inside a protective circle, or in any place the practitioners consider sacred, like wells and the locations of ancient Druidic gatherings.

References

O'Reilly, L. J. (2020, May 7). Paganism: Ireland's contemporary shining light. Trinity News. http://trinitynews.ie/2020/05/paganism-irelands-contemporary-shining-light/

Blakemore, E. (2019, November 15). Druids—facts and information. National Geographic. https://www.nationalgeographic.com/history/article/why-know-little-druids

Bollenbacher, S. (2012). The religion of the Irish Celts: Celtic paganism, Christianisation and Celtic Christianity. Grin Verlag.

Cartwright, M. (2021). Ancient Celtic religion. World History Encyclopedia. https://www.worldhistory.org/Ancient_Celtic_Religion/

Celtic Paganism, as seen by the. (n.d.). Celtic Druid Temple. https://www.celticdruidtemple.com/blog/celtic-paganism-as-seen-by-the-celtic-druid-temple.

Ede-Weaving, M. (2021, May 20). Ancestors of tradition. Order of Bards, Ovates & Druids. https://druidry.org/resources/ancestors-of-tradition

Irish Druids. (n.d.). Libraryireland.com. https://www.libraryireland.com/SocialHistoryAncientIreland/II-V-1.php

O'Reilly, L. J. (2020, May 7). Paganism: Ireland's contemporary shining light. Trinity News. http://trinitynews.ie/2020/05/paganism-irelands-contemporary-shining-light/

Patrick, S. (2017, November 30). Who were Celts. HISTORY. https://www.history.com/topics/ancient-history/celts

Roos, D. (2021, March 17). 8 facts about the Celts. HISTORY. https://www.history.com/news/celts-facts-ancient-europe

The Celts. (n.d.). TheSchoolRun. https://www.theschoolrun.com/homework-help/celts

The Editors of Encyclopedia Britannica. (2022). Druid. In Encyclopedia Britannica.

The Sacredness of Nature. (2012, March 22). The Druid Network. https://druidnetwork.org/what-is-druidry/beliefs-and-definitions/articles/the-sacredness-of-nature-an-article-by-phil-ryder/

What are Druids, Fili, and Bards? (2010, February 1). Celtic Studies Resources; Lisa Spangenberg. https://www.digitalmedievalist.com/opinionated-celtic-faqs/druids/

What is Celtic spirituality —. (n.d.). THE CELTIC CENTER. https://www.thecelticcenter.org/what-is-celtic-spirituality

Where did the Ancient Druids really come from? (n.d.). Gaia. https://www.gaia.com/article/who-were-the-ancient-druids

Who were the Druids? (2017, March 21). Historic UK. https://www.historic-uk.com/HistoryUK/HistoryofWales/Druids/

Berry, L. A. (2022, August 25). Who were the Druids? A history of Druidism in Britain. British Heritage. https://britishheritage.com/history/history-druids-britain

Who were the Druids? (2017, March 21). Historic UK. https://www.historic-uk.com/HistoryUK/HistoryofWales/Druids/

Beckett, J. (2014, October 12). The dark side of Druidry. John Beckett. https://www.patheos.com/blogs/johnbeckett/2014/10/the-dark-side-of-druidry.html

Cartwright, M. (2021). Death, burial & the afterlife in the ancient Celtic religion. World History Encyclopedia. https://www.worldhistory.org/article/1707/death-burial--the-afterlife-in-the-ancient-celtic/

Celtic religion - Beliefs, practices, and institutions. (n.d.). In Encyclopedia Britannica.

Cove, C. (2019, July 29). The Celtic Gods and Goddesses of ancient Ireland: The ultimate guide. ConnollyCove. https://www.connollycove.com/celtic-gods-goddesses-ancient-ireland/

Edition, I. (n.d.). The Pre-Christian Religion of Ancient Ireland – irishedition.com. Irishedition.com. https://irishedition.com/2017/08/the-pre-christian-religion-of-ancient-ireland/

Irish American Mom. (2012, November 26). Celtic religion. Irish American Mom; Irish American Mom LLC. https://www.irishamericanmom.com/celtic-religion/

Lambert, T. (2021, March 14). Celtic daily life. Local Histories. https://localhistories.org/celtic-daily-life/

Mark, J. J. (2015). Ancient Ireland. World History Encyclopedia. https://www.worldhistory.org/ireland/

Mulvihill, C. (2016, March 29). How nature shaped Celtic culture in Ireland. Green News Ireland. https://greennews.ie/how-nature-shaped-celtic-culture-in-ireland/

Neopaganism –. (n.d.). The Celtic Journey. https://thecelticjourney.wordpress.com/tag/neopaganism/

O'Brien, L. (2018a, September 25). Irish Pagan beliefs. Lora O'Brien - Irish Author & Guide; Lora O'Brien. https://loraobrien.ie/irish-pagan-beliefs/

O'Brien, L. (2018b, October 25). Irish pagan holidays. Lora O'Brien - Irish Author & Guide; Lora O'Brien. https://loraobrien.ie/irish-pagan-holidays/

Pagans in a Modern World: What is Neopaganism? (2017, March 11). Ancient Origins. https://www.ancient-origins.net/history-ancient-traditions/pagans-modern-world-what-neopaganism-007698

Snook, M. (2008). Of land, sea, and sky. Trafford Publishing.

Berry, L. A. (2022, August 25). Who were the Druids? A history of Druidism in Britain. British Heritage. https://britishheritage.com/history/history-druids-britain

Fields, K. (2018, December 10). Pagan afterlife: Where do pagans go when they die? Otherworldly Oracle; FIELDS CREATIVE CONSULTING. https://otherworldlyoracle.com/pagan-afterlife/

Bean chaointe. (2018, August 27). Bean Chaointe. https://beanchaointe.wordpress.com/2018/08/27/so-you-want-to-worship-the-morrigan/

Cartwright, M. (2021a). Lugh. World History Encyclopedia. https://www.worldhistory.org/Lugh/

Cartwright, M. (2021b). The Dagda. World History Encyclopedia. https://www.worldhistory.org/The_Dagda/

Cartwright, M. (2021c). The Mórrigan. World History Encyclopedia. https://www.worldhistory.org/The_Morrigan/

ConnollyCove. (2019, April 1). Morrigan: The fearless Celtic Goddess of War. ConnollyCove. https://www.connollycove.com/morrigan-goddess-of-war/

Emerick, C. (2016, February 14). The cailleach: Gaelic goddess of winter. Owlcation. https://owlcation.com/humanities/TheCailleach

Goddess cailleach bheur. (2012, December 22). Journeying to the Goddess. https://journeyingtothegoddess.wordpress.com/2012/12/22/goddess-cailleach-bheur/

How does one work with Lugh? (n.d.). Reddit. https://www.reddit.com/r/Paganacht/comments/cg7lsv/how_does_one_work_with_lugh/

Huanaco, F. (2021a, September 17). Morrígan: Goddess offerings, signs, symbols & myth. Spells8. https://spells8.com/lessons/goddess-morrigan-signs/

Huanaco, F. (2021b, October 10). Brigid: Goddess offerings, signs, symbols & myth. Spells8. https://spells8.com/lessons/brigid-goddess-symbols/

LetsGoIreland. (2022, May 9). Celtic gods & goddesses: The most important deities guide. Let's Go Ireland. https://www.letsgoireland.com/celtic-gods-and-celtic-goddesses/

LibGuides: The dagda: Giant god. (2020). https://westportlibrary.libguides.com/dagda

Offerings for the cailleach.... (2010, December 17). ....In the Chimehours. https://crookedways.wordpress.com/2010/12/17/offerings-for-the-cailleach/

O'Hara, K. (2022, May 21). The Morrigan: The story of the fiercest goddess in Irish myth. The Irish Road Trip. https://www.theirishroadtrip.com/the-morrigan/

Primal Heart. (n.d.). Devotional Practice to the Dagda –. Theprimalheart://theprimalheart.wordpress.com/category/the-dagda/devotional-practice-to-the-dagda/

Rhys, D. (2021, August 19). Lugh – ancient Celtic deity. Symbol Sage. https://symbolsage.com/lugh-celtic-mythology/

Turnbull, L. (2022, November 1). Brigid - Goddess of sun, fire, and childbirth. Goddess Gift; The Goddess Path. https://goddessgift.com/goddesses/brigid/

Wigington, P. (2007a, June 24). Lugh, master of skills. Learn Religions. https://www.learnreligions.com/lugh-master-of-skills-2561970

Wigington, P. (2007b, September 19). Brighid, the hearth goddess of Ireland. Learn Religions. https://www.learnreligions.com/brighid-hearth-goddess-of-ireland-2561958

Wigington, P. (2009, August 4). The Dagda, father god of Ireland. Learn Religions. https://www.learnreligions.com/the-dagda-father-god-of-ireland-2561706

Williams, A. (2020, August 16). Morrigan. Mythopedia. https://mythopedia.com/topics/morrigan

Woodfield, S. (2021, January 20). Connecting to the Morrigan as a goddess of prophecy. Llewellyn Worldwide. https://www.llewellyn.com/journal/article/2877

Wright, G. (2020a, August 16). Brigid. Mythopedia. https://mythopedia.com/topics/brigid

Wright, G. (2020b, August 16). Cailleach. Mythopedia. https://mythopedia.com/topics/cailleach

Wright, G. (2020c, August 16). Dagda. Mythopedia. https://mythopedia.com/topics/dagda

Wright, G. (2020d, August 16). Lugh. Mythopedia. https://mythopedia.com/topics/lugh

Aoibhell Fairy Queen of love. (n.d.). Emeraldisle.Ie. https://emeraldisle.ie/aoibhell-fairy-queen-of-love

Brent, H. (2019, August 22). Exploring Irish mythology: Clurichauns. The Irish Post. https://www.irishpost.com/life-style/exploring-irish-mythology-clurichauns-170462

Caitlin. (2021, September 7). Cat Sìth: including 5 Legendary Tales. Highland Titles. https://www.highlandtitles.com/blog/cat-sith/

Callan, P. D. (2019, September 20). IRISH MYTHOLOGICAL CREATURES: An A-Z guide and overview. Ireland Before You Die. https://www.irelandbeforeyoudie.com/an-a-z-guide-to-irish-mythological-creatures/

Connor. (2019, October 12). The Dullahan of Celtic mythology. The Irish Place. https://www.theirishplace.com/heritage/the-dullahan/

Cù sìth. (n.d.). Myths and Folklore Wiki. https://mythus.fandom.com/wiki/C%C3%B9_S%C3%ACth

Dobhar-chu. (n.d.). Cryptid Wiki. https://cryptidz.fandom.com/wiki/Dobhar-chu

Fear Gorta. (n.d.). Warriors Of Myth Wiki. https://warriorsofmyth.fandom.com/wiki/Fear_Gorta

Fowke, F. R. (1899). Gancanagh. Notes and Queries, s9-III(68), 297–297. https://doi.org/10.1093/nq/s9-iii.68.297d

Glaistig. (n.d.). Wikiwand. https://www.wikiwand.com/en/Glaistig

Irish folklore. (2016, April 12). Lullymore Heritage And Discovery Park | Leading Visitor Attraction | Pet Farm | School Tours | Crazy Golf | Train Trips. https://www.lullymoreheritagepark.com/fairy-village-lone-bush-folklore/

Jackman, N. (2021, March 26). The story of Abarta. Abarta Heritage Home. https://www.abartaheritage.ie/the-story-of-abarta/

Kneale, A. (2019, January 12). Magnificent horse of the Celtic gods - 'Enbarr of the Flowing Mane.' Transceltic - Home of the Celtic Nations. https://www.transceltic.com/pan-celtic/magnificent-horse-of-celtic-gods-enbarr-of-flowing-mane

Leanan Sidhe. (n.d.). Megami Tensei Wiki. https://megamitensei.fandom.com/wiki/Leanan_Sidhe

Leprechaun. (n.d.). Myths and Folklore Wiki. https://mythus.fandom.com/wiki/Leprechaun

Longáin, S. Ó. (2012, June 12). Pooka / púca in Irish folklore - legends in Irish Mythology & folklore. Your Irish Culture. https://www.yourirish.com/folklore/irish-pookas

Na Bocánaigh, Na bánánaigh. (2012, August 5). AN SIONNACH FIONN. https://ansionnachfionn.com/seanchas-mythology/na-bocanaigh-na-bananaigh/

Scott, K. (2021, May 30). The Irish folklore of the Celtic Merrow. Beachcombing Magazine.

https://www.beachcombingmagazine.com/blogs/news/the-irish-folklore-of-the-celtic-merrow

Surhone, L. M., Tennoe, M. T., & Henssonow, S. F. (Eds.). (2010). Oillipheist. Betascript Publishing.

The Bodach. (n.d.). Emeraldisle.Ie. https://emeraldisle.ie/the-bodach

The Editors of Encyclopedia Britannica. (2022). banshee. In Encyclopedia Britannica.

The Fomorians: Destructive giants of Irish legend. (2017, December 28). Ancient Origins. https://www.ancient-origins.net/myths-legends-europe/fomorians-destructive-giants-irish-legend-009349

Zhelyazkov, Y. (2021, June 7). Aos Sí – ancestors of Ireland. Symbol Sage. https://symbolsage.com/aos-si-ancestors-of-ireland/

The ossory werewolves. (n.d.). Kilkennycastle.Ie. https://kilkennycastle.ie/the-ossory-werewolves/

a lottery for tickets. (n.d.). Ancient Irish yule traditions. SCOIL RINCE LUIMNI. https://www.irishdancect.com/news/irish-history-volume-iii

Bhagat, D. (n.d.). The origins and practices of Litha. Bpl.org. https://www.bpl.org/blogs/post/the-origins-and-practices-of-litha/

Crawford, C. (2020, July 14). A beginners guide to the Wheel of the Year —. The Self-Care Emporium. https://theselfcareemporium.com/blog/beginners-guide-wheel-of-the-year

Dear, R. (1999). Celtic tree calendar: Your tree sign and you. Souvenir Press.

Mark, J. J. (2019). Wheel of the Year. World History Encyclopedia. https://www.worldhistory.org/Wheel_of_the_Year/

Moody, S. (n.d.). Meanwhile, in Ireland: Ostara. The Comenian https://comenian.org/7527/news/meanwhile-in-ireland-ostara/

Samhain (samain) - the Celtic roots of Halloween. (n.d.). Newgrange.com. https://www.newgrange.com/samhain.htm

Soul, M. M. (2019). Imbolc: Witch's Journal & Workbook. Independently Published.

The Editors of Encyclopedia Britannica. (2018). Belenus. In Encyclopedia Britannica.

The Pagan Grimoire. (2020, April 18th). The Wheel of the Year: The 8 festivals in the Wiccan calendar. The Pagan Grimoire. https://www.pagangrimoire.com/wheel-of-the-year/

The Wheel of the Year: the calendar of pagan festivals explained. (n.d.). Sky HISTORY TV Channel. https://www.history.co.uk/articles/the-wheel-of-the-year-the-calendar-of-pagan-festivals-explained

Wigington, P. (2007a, May 13). History of Yule. Learn Religions. https://www.learnreligions.com/history-of-yule-2562997

Wigington, P. (2007b, November 26). All About Yule. Learn Religions. https://www.learnreligions.com/all-about-yule-2562972

Wigington, P. (2008a, January 4). All About Imbolc. Learn Religions. https://www.learnreligions.com/guide-to-celebrating-imbolc-2562102

Wigington, P. (2008b, February 25). Celebrating Ostara, the Spring Equinox. Learn Religions. https://www.learnreligions.com/all-about-ostara-the-spring-equinox-2562471

Wigington, P. (2008c, May 20). Celebrating Litha, the summer solstice. Learn Religions. https://www.learnreligions.com/guide-to-celebrating-litha-2562231

Wigington, P. (2008d, July 9). All About Lammas (Lughnasadh). Learn Religions. https://www.learnreligions.com/celebrating-lammas-or-lughnasadh-in-august-2562156

Wigington, P. (2008e, August 14). Mabon: The autumn equinox. Learn Religions. https://www.learnreligions.com/all-about-mabon-the-autumn-equinox-2562286

Wigington, P. (2008f, August 22). All About Samhain. Learn Religions. https://www.learnreligions.com/all-about-samhain-2562691

Wigington, P. (2011, September 18). Celtic tree months. Learn Religions. https://www.learnreligions.com/celtic-tree-months-2562403

Wright, G. (2020, August 16th). Lugh. Mythopedia. https://mythopedia.com/topics/lugh

O'Brien, L. (2018, October 22). An Irish Pagan Altar - Lora O'Brien - Irish Author & Guide. Lora O'Brien - Irish Author & Guide. https://loraobrien.ie/irish-pagan-altar/

Wigington, P. (n.d.). 14 Magical Tools for Pagan Practice. Learn Religions. https://www.learnreligions.com/magical-tools-for-pagan-practice-4064607

Wigington, P. (n.d.). Magical Crystals and Gemstones. Learn Religions. https://www.learnreligions.com/magical-crystals-and-gemstones-2562758

Wigington, P. (n.d.). The Magic & Symbolism of Animals. Learn Religions. https://www.learnreligions.com/the-magic-of-animals-2562522

What Do Pagans Do? (n.d.). Pluralism.Org. https://pluralism.org/what-do-pagans-do

Wigington, P. (n.d.). Beltane Rites and Rituals. Learn Religions. https://www.learnreligions.com/beltane-rites-and-rituals-2561678

Irish Healing Waters Spell. (n.d.). Ecauldron.Net. https://www.ecauldron.net/spells/heal04.php

Ancient Irish spells and charms to celebrate Halloween. (2022, October 29). IrishCentral.Com. http://www.irishcentral.com/roots/the-magic-of-irish-witches-and-druids-top-ten-ancient-irish-charms-and-spells-128912303-237762261.html

Belladonna, R. (2019, September 17). A Spell For Love and Unity. A Trans Witch Grimoire. https://medium.com/a-trans-witch-grimoire/a-spell-for-love-and-unity-f8de2582c7ff

O'Brien, L. (2018, September 25). Irish Pagan Beliefs. Lora O'Brien - Irish Author & Guide. https://loraobrien.ie/irish-pagan-beliefs/

O'Reilly, L. J. (2020, May 7). Paganism: Ireland's contemporary shining light. Trinity News. http://trinitynews.ie/2020/05/paganism-irelands-contemporary-shining-light/